ALL AROUND THE WORLD
PAKISTAN

by Kristine Spanier, MLIS

Ideas for Parents and Teachers

Pogo Books let children practice reading informational text while introducing them to nonfiction features such as headings, labels, sidebars, maps, and diagrams, as well as a table of contents, glossary, and index.

Carefully leveled text with a strong photo match offers early fluent readers the support they need to succeed.

Before Reading

- "Walk" through the book and point out the various nonfiction features. Ask the student what purpose each feature serves.
- Look at the glossary together. Read and discuss the words.

Read the Book

- Have the child read the book independently.
- Invite him or her to list questions that arise from reading.

After Reading

- Discuss the child's questions. Talk about how he or she might find answers to those questions.
- Prompt the child to think more. Ask: Pakistan has both deserts and mountains. What landforms are near you?

Pogo Books are published by Jump!
5357 Penn Avenue South
Minneapolis, MN 55419
www.jumplibrary.com

Library of Congress Cataloging-in-Publication Data

Names: Spanier, Kristine, author.
Title: Pakistan / Kristine Spanier.
Description: Minneapolis, MN: Jump!, Inc., 2021.
Series: All around the world | Includes index.
Audience: 7-10 | Audience: 2-3
Identifiers: LCCN 2019045721 (print)
LCCN 2019045722 (ebook)
ISBN 9781645273479 (hardcover)
ISBN 9781645273486 (paperback)
ISBN 9781645273493 (ebook)
Subjects: LCSH: Pakistan—Juvenile literature.
Classification: LCC DS376.9 .S725 2021 (print)
LCC DS376.9 (ebook) | DDC 954.91—dc23
LC record available at https://lccn.loc.gov/2019045721
LC ebook record available at https://lccn.loc.gov/2019045722

Editor: Jenna Gleisner
Designer: Molly Ballanger

Photo Credits: Burhan Ay/Shutterstock, cover, 17; Matthew Richard/Shutterstock, 1; Pixfiction/Shutterstock, 3; MaRabelo/iStock, 4; Pawika Tongtavee/Shutterstock, 5; ARTISTIDIS VAFEIADAKIS/Alamy, 6-7; rashid/Getty 8-9; rabia.irfan/Shutterstock, 10; Pises Tungittipokai/Shutterstock, 11; khlongwangchao/Shutterstock, 12-13; Mikhail Semenov/Shutterstock, 14-15tl; Warren Metcalf/Shutterstock, 14-15tr; Miroslav Hlavko/Shutterstock, 14-15bl; Nilanjan Chatterjee/Alamy, 14-15br; Faraz Hyder Jafri/Shutterstock, 16; Friedrich Stark/Alamy, 18-19; Pacific Press Agency/Alamy, 20-21; Arfan Afzal/Shutterstock, 23.

Printed in the United States of America at Corporate Graphics in North Mankato, Minnesota.

TABLE OF CONTENTS

CHAPTER 1

WELCOME TO PAKISTAN!

K2

Would you like to see the world's second tallest mountain? This is K2. It is 28,251 feet (8,611 meters) high! People have climbed it from Pakistan!

Petroglyphs are outside of Chilās. Some are 2,700 years old. Welcome!

petroglyph

Many people in Pakistan are Muslim. They celebrate Ramadan. Eid al-Fitr is at the end of Ramadan. It lasts three days. People give gifts to one another. Girls and women may decorate themselves with **mehndi**.

WHAT DO YOU THINK?

Eid al-Adha is another festival. People share food with others during this time. What holidays do you celebrate? How do you celebrate them?

mehndi

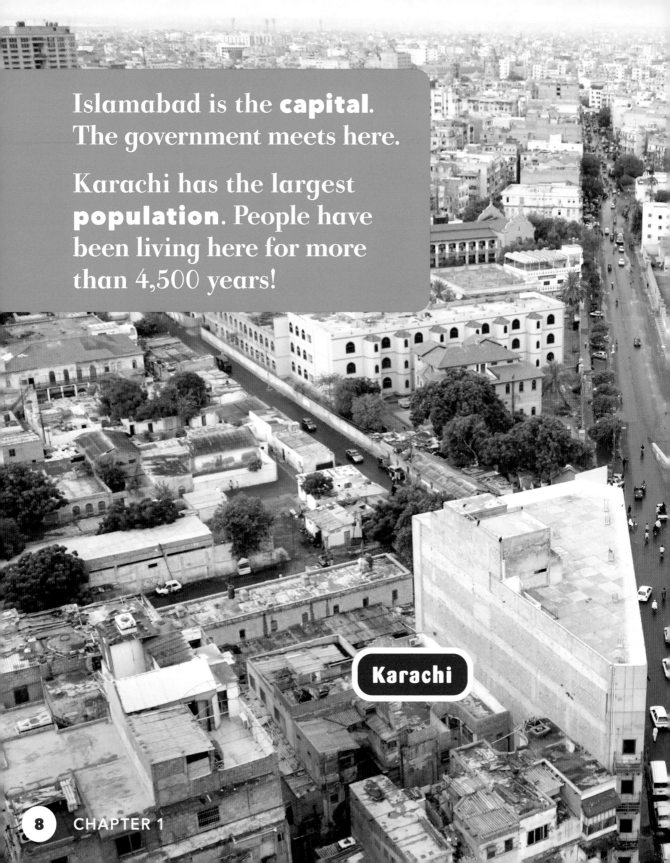

Islamabad is the **capital**. The government meets here.

Karachi has the largest **population**. People have been living here for more than 4,500 years!

Karachi

TAKE A LOOK!

Green is a **sacred** color of Islam. It is on the country's flag. It stands for Pakistan's Muslim people. People of other religions are included, too. What do the **symbols** on the flag mean?

■ = Muslim people
□ = non-Muslim people
☾ moon = **progress**
☆ star = light and knowledge

CHAPTER 2

LAND AND ANIMALS

The Thar Desert borders Pakistan and India. Temperatures can reach 120 degrees Fahrenheit (49 degrees Celsius)! Hot winds blow.

Thar Desert

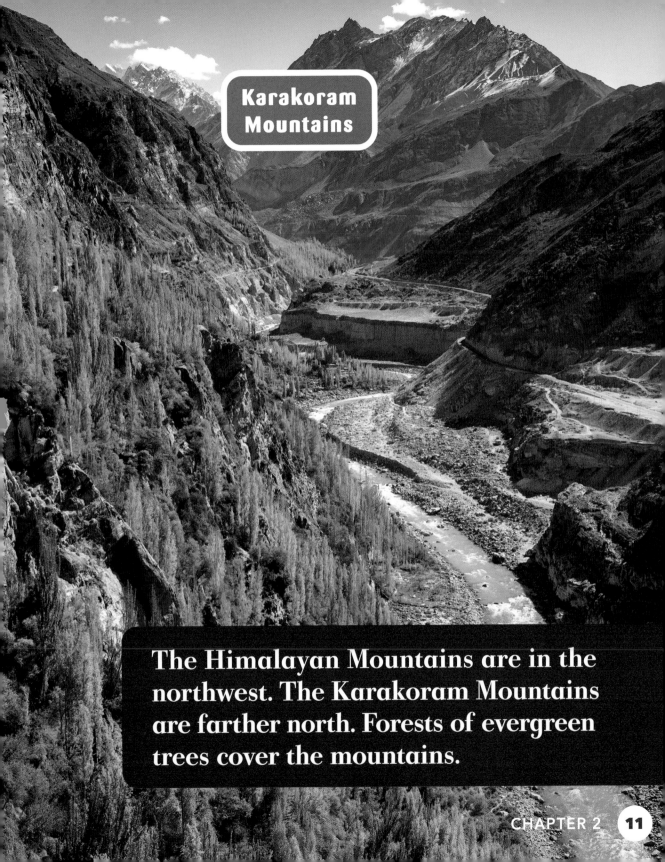

Karakoram Mountains

The Himalayan Mountains are in the northwest. The Karakoram Mountains are farther north. Forests of evergreen trees cover the mountains.

The Indus River **Valley** has rich farmland. **Crops** grow well here. Cotton, wheat, rice, and sugarcane are some. Floods are common between July and August. This is the **monsoon** season.

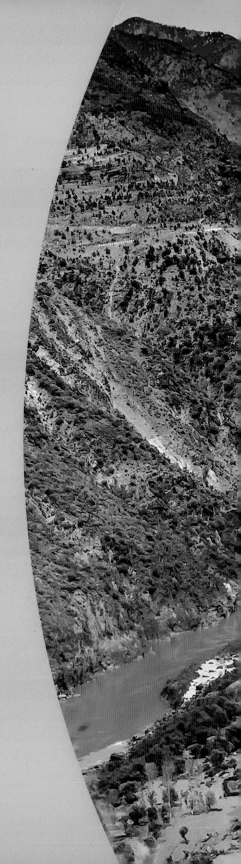

Indus River

rice crop

markhor

snow leopard

wild boar

river dolphin

Markhors and snow leopards live in the mountains. Wild boars live near the Indus River. The river is home to freshwater dolphins.

WHAT DO YOU THINK?

People have added **dams** to the Indus River. This helps with **irrigation**. But it has affected the **habitat** of the dolphin. Do you think the homes of animals should be protected?

CHAPTER 3

LIFE IN PAKISTAN

Food here is spicy. It is cooked with **curry**. Chapati is a flat pita bread. Rice is served with many meals. Biryani is a meat and rice dish. Lassi is a creamy drink.

biryani

Artists create bright designs. You can see it on wood, stones, and leather. People also paint trucks!

It is hard to go to school in Pakistan. Why? Many **rural** schools don't have electricity or water. City schools get more money from the government. Some families travel to cities so kids can go to school there.

DID YOU KNOW?

Girls here are sometimes discouraged from attending school. Malala Yousafzai grew up here. She is now famous. Why? She stood up for girls' rights to education. She won the Nobel Peace Prize!

People play many kinds of sports here. Cricket is popular. So is polo. Kho-kho is a game of tag. It is played in teams. Kabaddi is another game of tag. But players must hold their breath while chasing others!

There is much to see in Pakistan. Would you like to learn even more?

polo

QUICK FACTS & TOOLS

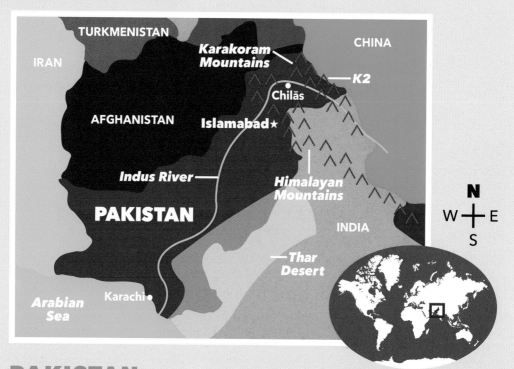

PAKISTAN

Location: southern Asia

Size: 307,374 square miles (796,095 square kilometers)

Population: 207,862,518 (July 2018 estimate)

Capital: Islamabad

Type of Government: federal parliamentary republic

Languages: Punjabi, Sindhi, Saraiki, Pashto, Urdu, Balochi, Hindko, Brahui, English Burushaski

Exports: textiles, rice, leather, chemicals

Currency: Pakistani Rupee

GLOSSARY

capital: A city where government leaders meet.

crops: Plants grown for food.

curry: A powder with a hot, spicy taste, made from various spices.

dams: Barriers across streams or rivers that hold back water.

habitat: The place where an animal or plant is usually found.

irrigation: The method of supplying water to crops by artificial means, such as channels and pipes.

mehndi: A form of body art that originated in India and includes decorative designs.

monsoon: A storm that brings heavy rain.

petroglyphs: Carvings in rock.

population: The total number of people who live in a place.

progress: A forward movement or improvement.

rural: Related to the country and country life.

sacred: Holy, having to do with religion, or very important and deserving of respect.

symbols: Objects or designs that stand for, suggest, or represent something else.

valley: A low area of land between two hills or mountains, often containing a river or stream.

Pakistan's currency

INDEX

TO LEARN MORE

Finding more information is as easy as 1, 2, 3.

1. Go to www.factsurfer.com
2. Enter "Pakistan" into the search box.
3. Click the "Surf" button to see a list of websites.

FACT SURFER